For you,
Happy Reading!

ISBN: 9798372103085

Growing Readers

All rights reserved

A IS FOR APPLE

T. Paris

apple

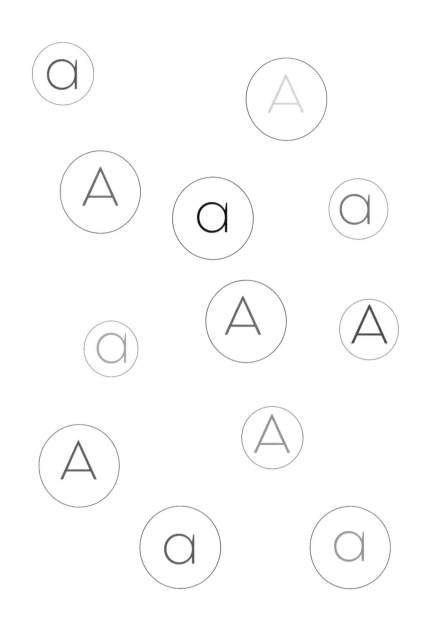

Apple

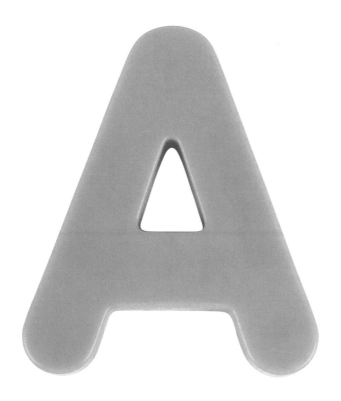

Apple

Apple

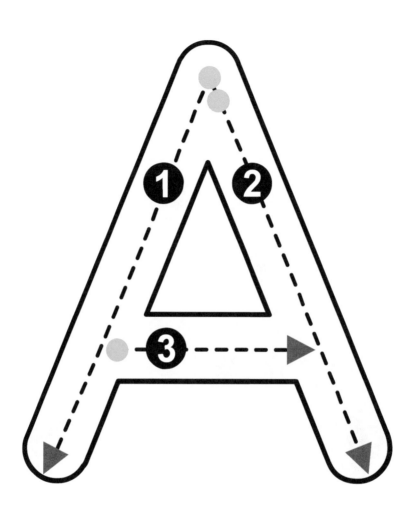

Apple

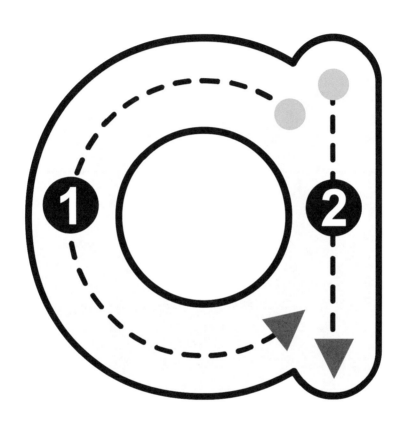

apple

Apple

apple

a A

A a

a A

Apple

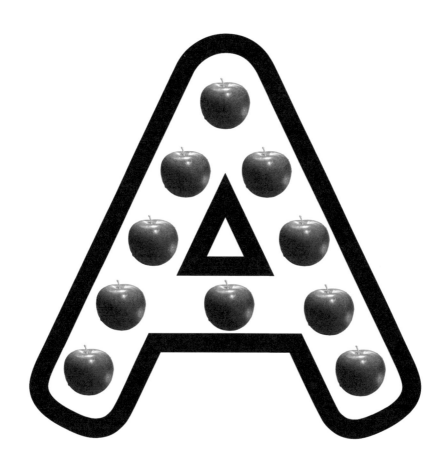

Apples!

Made in the USA
Columbia, SC
05 March 2024

32568948R00015